ABCs
with
Jesus and Me

Twenty-Six Letters in the Alphabet
Twenty-Six Devotions
All Are Welcome Here

Nikki Plummer

ISBN 979-8-89345-913-5 (paperback)
ISBN 979-8-89345-915-9 (digital)

Christian Faith Publishing
832 Park Avenue
Meadville, PA 16335
www.christianfaithpublishing.com

Printed in the United States of America

To the lost who want to be found.
To the person craving to feel a love that never ends.
To the person needing to be set free.

Note from the Author

I am not perfect, and I am flawed, but I am forgiven and freed from my past and all the pain I've ever felt. If you are reading this and do not know Jesus yet or are struggling with your relationship with Him, know that I am praying for you. I was you. I was the person who didn't know where to start or didn't believe I was worthy enough to be redeemed from my past. Through this devotional, I pray the chains will fall off you as fast as they were put on. Jesus heals all, loves all, and conquers all. He saved my life, and I know He can save yours too.

You can work through this at your own pace. You can do this as a twenty-six-day or twenty-six-week devotional. I recommend using a separate journal or notebook so you can answer the journal prompts in each section. Let's get started!

Contents

Anger

Noun

A strong feeling of annoyance, displeasure, or hostility

What does God say about anger?

> For man's anger does not bring about the righteous life that God desires. (James 1:20)

> A hot-tempered man stirs up strife, but he who is slow to anger quiets contention. (Proverbs 15:18)

What are you angry about right now? Is there something that you are constantly thinking about that causes you to not have peace? Write it out.

_____

_____

_____

How long have you been angry about what you listed above?

_____

Journal prompt

Is there a reason you are still holding on to this anger you feel? Is someone else constantly making you angry or upsetting you? Is it something within your own heart?

Spend the next few minutes reflecting on these questions, and write out any thoughts in your journal.

Now, what if I told you that you don't have to hold on to this anger? Sounds simple, right? I will be the first to tell you that letting things go does not come easy for me. I have held on to hurt for so long that it eventually became "normal" in my life, and I believed that it was never going to get better. Then I found Jesus, and He rescued me from the metaphorical chains I had around myself and others. I am still working on letting things go from my past, but I have a friend and Father who is always here to listen and help me let things go in His time, not mine.

Often, the anger we feel is just hurt that hasn't been released or dealt with. Anger builds up because we don't have a way to release it or truly heal from the root of the problem. If we try to heal by ourselves, we are always going to be let down. Today, give your burden(s) to Jesus. Ask Him to release these burdens from your soul and lift the weight off your shoulders. He does miraculous things and heals the brokenhearted. If He can heal the anger in me, He can heal the anger in you.

Let's pray

Lord, I pray today for the person reading this, for the person who is holding on to anger from their past, and for the person who is holding on to anger within themselves and the things they've done. I pray You will give them Your peace and let them understand You forgive the messiest of situations, and You don't hold anger or hurt against us. Lord, be merciful to the person reading this. I pray You will be with the people who have made us angry in our lives, that You will bless them and reveal Your goodness to them. Lord, fix and heal our angry hearts so we don't have to feel angst anymore. Help us to know anger does *not* come from You. *We are more than the feelings we feel.*

Do you feel like you can let the anger go? If not, memorize the scriptures at the beginning of this section and diligently pray God will renew your heart. If you do feel better, remember, healing takes time, and every day your heart will heal more and more if you let God intervene.

> Do not be too quick to get angry because anger lives in the fool's heart. (Ecclesiastes 7:9)

Betrayal

Noun

The action of betraying one's country, a group, or a person; treachery

> Do not take revenge, my dear friends, but leave room for God's wrath, for it is written: "It is mine to avenge; I will repay," says the Lord. (Romans 12:19)

> Your relatives, members of your own family-even they have betrayed you; they have raised a loud cry against you. Do not trust them, though they speak well of you. (Jeremiah 12:6)

Has someone you love betrayed you? Has someone you've barely known betrayed you or brought you down? I am guessing, at some point in your life, you have felt betrayed. Often, the people we are closest to are the ones who hurt us most. Who has betrayed you? Write their name(s) below.

_____

Was it hard to write their names down? Sometimes it can be hard to write their names on paper because it makes us feel vulnerable. I have felt betrayed several times throughout my life. I have always taken it personally and have believed that the other person has to apologize for me to move on and forgive them. The more I read Jesus's Word, the more I realize that betrayal has a lot less to do with the person who betrayed me and a lot more to do with my own heart. There are people who intentionally hurt others, but there are also people who are hurting, and their hurting causes a chain reaction of events that leads to someone else getting hurt. Our Healer can heal this form of betrayal. When someone betrays us, especially a loved one, we often feel offended and take it personally. This offense leads to us pushing them away, saying things we don't mean, or it leaves us with bitterness in our hearts. What if instead of feeling betrayed, we took a moment to try and understand why the other person did what they did? Have they been hurt? Are they holding onto things from their past that are causing them to deflect their problems onto us? Are they insecure? Are they crying out for help?

Journal prompt

Write out what happened to you. Write the betrayal that keeps coming to your mind while reading this.

Now that you have written down the betrayal you've felt, do you think that the person who betrayed you has felt betrayed too? They may not feel betrayed by you but by someone else in their past. Regardless of how hurt you are and how much pain they caused, do you believe they should be forgiven? Circle one.

○ Yes

○ No

I hope you circled yes. If you circled no, it is okay. We may not think they should be forgiven or we may want to get revenge/justice, but Jesus tells us that we are *all* forgiven, and in time, you will realize that your offender deserves forgiveness, just like you. Remember, when you forgive others, you too are forgiven. Harboring hurt keeps us in a stationary position. Forgiveness keeps us moving forward.

> When they kept on questioning him, he straightened up and said to them, "Let any one of you who is without sin be the first to throw a stone at her." (John 8:7)

Are you without sin? Circle one below.

○ Yes

○ No

There is a correct answer to this question and it is *no*.

> We have all sinned and fall short of God's glory.
> (Romans 3:23)

Since we are all sinners and all fall short, we have to let go of the things that are done to us by others. We have to let go of betrayal and hurt, not for the person who betrayed us but for the person inside of us wanting to feel whole again. Like I said before, I have been betrayed, and I have carried that hurt for way too long. I have let betrayal dictate my life and how I treat the person who betrayed me. I wanted justice, an apology, an acceptance of the hurt they caused. But most of the time, these things don't happen. What *is* offered to you and me is forgiveness from our Father, who loves us and forgives us, for holding a grudge against the person(s). He gives guidance on how to forgive them completely.

Again, write the name(s) of the person(s) that has/have betrayed you.

_____

I believe that the more you write and say their names, the easier it is to let go of the hurt you feel. You may not ever have the same relationship with them as you did before the hurt. You may never hear an apology, but you can have peace in your heart, knowing you let the grudge you were holding on to not have a grasp on your heart anymore.

Let's pray

Lord, we come to You in prayer today for the people who have betrayed us in our life, for the people who were once close to us and let us down. We pray that You bless them. We pray You will heal the brokenness and help us to not hold a grudge against them. We pray for understanding and a humbleness that helps us to realize that none of us are perfect, and we all have fallen short of Your goodness and glory. We pray You will not only heal our hearts but the hearts of our offenders. Help us to work on loving them and help remind us that we all have a story. We all have hurt and heartache, but not all of us have You. Be with the people who don't know You and who are left alone in this world. We pray they will find You, seek You, and know You. We pray with the forgiveness You have given us that we can forgive others who have hurt us. Jesus, help us to show Your love through the way we treat people who have offended us.

Mirror, Mirror

The burdens are heavy, and my mind runs wild,
but if I know Jesus, the stress should be mild.

How do I let all this hurt go,
when I'm afraid it's all I'll ever know.
How do you forgive someone who doesn't show remorse,
someone who constantly takes you down the same dreaded course,
someone who makes you feel of little worth,
someone who doesn't appreciate your birth?

How do you release the anger and fear
so that you can be happy again when you look in the mirror?

My friend, the mirror is a magical place,
a place to show you your own individual face,
a place to look and see what God created!
He made you perfect in His own way; it's amazing, ain't it?

Now, friend, fix your eyes not on others but on the Lord.
Don't you see? He's created you for so much more.

You were created for more than the words others speak or the days
where you feel so very weak.

Now listen here, my friend.
The way you forgive is to let it go,
to make sure your heart is free, ya know.

Release your hurt and your burdens too.
Give them to Jesus because He knows what to do.

God loves you with unconditional grace,
so look in the mirror and put that smile back on your face!

C

Consistency

Noun

Conformity in the application of something, typically that which is necessary for the sake of logic, accuracy, and fairness

> Stand firm and don't be shaken, always keep busy working for the Lord. You know that everything you do for him is worthwhile. (1 Corinthians 15:58)

> Let us not become weary in doing good, for at the proper time we will reap a harvest if we do not give up. (Galatians 6:9)

In all honesty, consistency has been something I've always struggled with. I will start something but eventually give it up and move on to the next thing. I have a hard time staying focused and committed. For the last ten years of my life, one of the only things that has remained consistent in my life is Jesus. I did not grow up with Jesus in my heart or my life. After learning about Him in college and being exposed to His Word, I began to actively seek Him. My faith has wavered, I have sinned, and I am far from perfect, but He's remained consistent. He has been there for me through it all and has never left my side. His love, forgiveness, and grace have all been a constant in my life, and it has given me courage to be more consistent with the things I start and want to finish. Is there something you've wanted to do or started and then stopped? Write it out.

_____

_____

_____

Journal prompt

What is stopping you from starting, or what stopped you initially from carrying it out? Is it finances? Was your heart not into it? Were you told you couldn't do it? Did you tell yourself you couldn't do it?

Jesus tells us, "Do not conform to the pattern of this world but be transformed by the renewing of your mind" (Romans 12:2).

Train your mind to believe in yourself. When you feel like giving up, go to God's Word. Let Him remind you that you can do all things through Him who gives you strength (Philippians 4:13).

Whether it is something like sticking to a workout plan or reading God's Word every morning before you start your day, ask God to help you stay consistent. Ask God to bring His constant help in your life so you can have consistency in the things you strive to do.

Let's pray

Today, I want you to write out your own prayer in your journal. I want you to pray for God's consistency in your life so that you can be consistent in your relationships and the things you do.

Darkness

Noun
The partial or total absence of light

> This is the message we have heard from him and declare to you: God is light; in him there is no darkness at all. If we claim to have fellowship with him and yet walk in the darkness, we lie and do not live out the truth. But if we walk in the light, as he is in the light, we have fellowship with one another, and the blood of Jesus, his Son, purifies us from all sin. (1 John 1:5–7)

Can you look back on a time in your life where you felt the darkness overtaking you? You may be experiencing this right now while reading this. Whether you felt the weight of the darkness years ago or you are feeling it right now, you are not alone. Darkness has never overcome God's light. You may feel like you can't see the light at the end of your pain and hurt right now, but Jesus promises to walk through it with us. His light shines brighter than any darkness around us.

> Even when we walk through the darkest valley, we should not fear because He is there to comfort us. (Psalm 23:4)

If you don't know Jesus or have never been saved and have been living in darkness all your life, the prayer at the end of today's devotion is for you. I lived in darkness for eighteen years. I felt all of the weight from my grief and suffering every single day. I had no peace in my life, and I constantly was looking for anything to fill the void I felt. I searched for years to find what could make me feel whole, and I finally found it in the Word of Jesus. If you know Jesus but are walking through a dark time right now, remember, He will carry you through. You are not alone, and your pain and suffering are valid. It's okay to cry; it's okay to have bad days, and it's okay to not feel your best. Just remember, at the end of every day, to thank Jesus for all He has done for you and all He will continue to do. He will heal your pain and take the weight of your burden off your shoulders if you will let Him.

Always remember, as the night turns black each and every night, the sun rises each and every morning. There is always light that comes after the darkness. There is always freedom from our pain. There is always hope for a better tomorrow.

Journal prompt

What do you need to release today? Write it out.

Let's pray

Lord, I pray to You today for the people who don't know Your love and Your compassion. I pray You forgive the person reading this, and I pray they will come to You on their knees, asking for Your light to shine in their life. Please reveal Yourself to them and overcome the darkness in their life with the light of Your word and truth. Please help them to know they are worthy of Your love, and they are never too far from You. Nothing they have ever done can keep them from feeling Your freedom and Your peace. Please help them to surrender their life to You so they can walk into their future with hope and healing. Lord, be with those who are walking through a dark time right now, whether it be the grief of losing a loved one, the pain of this world, and all the hurt it can cause, the end of a relationship, losing sight of who they are, or a disease they are battling. Guide them, and be with them. Hold their hand, and walk alongside them through their journey. I pray they have courage to know You are a miracle worker, and You keep Your promises to Your children. Let anyone who doesn't know You come to You and seek Your love. Make Your light shine brighter than any darkness that is trying to overtake them. Satan fights hard, but You always win. Lord, shine Your bright light on our darkest days so we are always reminded that You are in control of our lives.

I Wish I Knew

I wish I knew what to say to someone like you.

Someone who is grieving over the loss of a parent or loved one
and doesn't know what to do.

My earthly words may be of little comfort,
but our God in heaven is triumphant.

He can take your tears and pain,
just like that crimson stain He washed away.

I want you to know to keep holding on
to the promises we've been told for so long.

One day, all our pain will go away,
but for now, we have been chosen here to stay.

So as you stay,
Please look up and not away!
Look up to the one who made you
and to the one who is going to get you through.

You are stronger than your hardest days,
and don't forget you can always go to God and pray.

Hang on, my friend,
this pain and grief is not your end!

Envy

Noun

A feeling of discontented or resentful longing aroused by someone else's possessions, qualities, or luck

Does reading this definition make you feel uneasy? It makes my heart heavy for those of us that compare our lives and what we have to those around us. Let's see what Jesus says about envy.

> We do not dare classify or compare ourselves with some who commend themselves. When they measure themselves by themselves and compare themselves with themselves, they are not wise. (2 Corinthians 10:12)

We all have burdens we carry, and we all have our own struggles we don't tell anyone about. When we compare our lives to others, we lose the ability to be who God uniquely made us to be. We are all different, but we are all the same. As humans, we all feel pain, joy, love, loss, hope, fear, resentment, and contentment. In reality, we only get a small glimpse into other people's lives. We may see a small snapshot of others' lives on the Internet or in our small group at church or when we go to a social gathering, but we don't live in their house, and we don't see what happens every moment of their day. We typically don't see people at their worst. We often see a highlight reel of the good. We don't see the suffering that people go through when the doors are closed and the cameras are turned off.

There is always going to be something we wish we had: a bigger house, a better job, a bigger bank account, a trendier closet, a bigger group of friends, more followers on social media, more attention in the community, etc. Philippians 4:19 states, "And my God will meet all your needs according to the riches of his glory in Christ Jesus."

God gives us everything we need when we need it. All the things listed above are worldly items that have no worth in eternity. Having a roof over our heads, food on our table, and jobs that provide a stable income are incredibly large blessings we often take for granted. Do not be envious of those who have more than you. Who are we to decide what possessions are worth? Our salvation and spending eternity with Jesus is worth more than everything else this world has to offer.

Stop comparing your life to others, and start thanking God for all that you have. Below, write down five things you are thankful for.

① _____

② _____

③ _____

④ _____

⑤ _____

Now, write down five things you *wish* you had.

① _____

② _____

③ _____

④ _____

⑤ _____

With both of your lists above, remember, the only thing in life we truly need (besides shelter, clothing, food, and water) is a relationship with God. Most of our wish lists are things we *want* and not necessarily things we *need* to live our day to day lives. If all we have is Jesus, we have more than enough. Stop letting the world misguide your perception on what you have or don't have. Start thanking Jesus every day for what he has given you so you can feel refreshed, knowing you have everything you need. God made you just the way you are for a reason. Though you may feel your differences or your unique traits are the things that make you less worthy than someone else, remember, God created mankind in His own image (Genesis 1:27). He made you exactly the way you are supposed to be.

Do not be envious of what someone else may have that you don't because, likely, you have something that they wish they had.

Let's pray.

Lord, help us to not compare ourselves to others. Help us to be at peace with exactly how You made us to be. Let us see beauty in our flaws and imperfections of who we are and what makes us unique. I pray the person reading this knows how loved they are for exactly who You've made them to be. Fix our eyes on You so we will stop comparing ourselves to everyone around us and start listening to what Your Word says about who we are. Our joy and happiness come from our relationship with You, and no worldly possession can ever make up for that. Lord, help us to surrender all we have to You today and help us to stop comparing ourselves to one another. Let us love who we are so in return we can love others the way You have loved us.

Fear

Noun

An unpleasant emotion caused by the belief that someone or something is dangerous, likely to cause pain, or a threat

The enemy uses fear to control us and our emotions. When fear and the enemy creep in, here are some Bible verses to read and memorize.

> So do not fear, for I am with you; do not be dismayed, for I am your God. I will strengthen you and help you; I will uphold you with my righteous right hand. (Isaiah 41:10)

> Who of you by worrying can add a single hour to your life? Since you cannot do this very little thing, why do you worry about the rest? (Luke 12:25–26)

> The Lord your God is with you, the Mighty Warrior who saves. He will take great delight in you; in his love he will no longer rebuke you, but will rejoice over you with singing. (Zephaniah 3:17)

> Overhearing what they said, Jesus told him, "Don't be afraid; just believe." (Mark 5:36)

Fear creeps in like a roaring lion. We all have something that scares us or causes fearful emotions every time we do it. For me, it is flying. I do not enjoy it, and it causes me a great deal of anxiety every time I fly somewhere. Before the plane takes off, I always recite Joshua 1:9: "Have I not commanded you? Be strong and courageous. Do not be afraid; do not be discouraged, for the Lord your God will be with you wherever you go." No amount of worrying can change whatever we are facing or are scared of. It is as simple as that. It's hard to train our brains to not worry. Every corner you turn, every chapter in your life, everywhere you look, there is something you can be worrying about. Just because you *can* be worrying about it, doesn't mean you *should* be. Training our minds to memorize scripture helps to ease us in times of distress. Fear can overwhelm and consume us in an instant if we don't have something to battle against it. On our own, we are weak. But with Jesus, we are strong and can have peace in the most difficult and fearful situations.

Journal prompt

What is one thing you constantly fear or something that scares you?

_____

Do you have a scripture you recite in your head when you are fearful or worried?

○ Yes

○ No

If you said no, look at the scriptures above and write down the one that brings you the most peace when you read it.

_____

_____

_____

_____

For some of you, it is not something you fear but someone. You may have been hurt by someone and are fearful of him or her and what he or she may do to you. If this is you, take a moment right now to pray that God will release the chains from you and the person who hurt you. Pray you can forgive them. Say their name out loud, and ask God to capture their heart and yours. Ask God for His redemption, peace, forgiveness, and salvation.

A reminder: Just because you forgive someone and let him or her out of your grasp does *not* mean you have to allow that person to keep hurting you. Forgiving them heals you and helps you move forward. If you can keep them in your life and rebuild the relationship, great! If you have to love the person from a distance for either your safety or emotional reasons, let the grasp of bitterness and hurt leave your soul so both of you can be free from the pain that was caused. Let only Jesus have a stronghold on your life. Surrender everything to Jesus, and let Him transform your heart so you can be made new in His image.

> The Lord is my light and my salvation—whom shall I fear? The Lord is the stronghold of my life—of whom shall I be afraid? (Psalm 27:1)

Let's pray

Lord, I pray for the fearful today. I pray for those who have something that makes them worry or fear every time they face it. I pray they will remember that their strength comes from You and that You are in control at all times. Nothing we do, no amount of worrying, and no amount of fear can drive out Your perfect will for us. Help our hearts to be still in Your presence, and help us to worry less and praise You more for the good things You are doing in our life. Worrying causes so much extra heartache and pain. Remind us that Your Word is a safe place for us to go when our worrying gets out of control.

For the person who has been hurt and is fearful of someone else or who fears the person they've become because of their pain, guard their hearts from bitterness and emptiness. Change their perspective, Lord. Give them courage to read Your Word every day so that pain from the past can be released from the hold they have on it. First John 4:18 says, "There is no fear in love. But perfect love drives out fear, because fear has to do with punishment. The one who fears is not made perfect in love." Drive out fear today, Lord, so we can live for You, and let You live through us. Our fear causes pain, and Your love brings peace. Let our fear dissipate, and help our hearts to find comfort in Your Word.

To the person that needs to hear this, who needs to let the past go, who needs to let go of the chains you've put around yourself and others; to those of you that need to feel God's presence and that need to forgive yourself and others; to those of you that need hope and need to say goodbye to fear, this poem is for you.

When Fear Creeps In

When fear creeps in,
my hope escapes.
My fear seems to take me to a different place.
A place where no one wants to go,
and definitely a place we rarely show.

We don't show others our hurt and pain,
because we are afraid.
Afraid they might judge,
or even drag our names through the mud.

Be honest with yourselves and others too,
because that is what we are called to do.

It doesn't matter what others think or believe,
because greater is the one who lives in me.

God tells us who we are and what we can do;
don't let anyone ever steal that from you.

Fear can close door after door.
Honesty can open doors and help you move forward.

Choose to release your fear today.
Be honest with yourself and pray.
Pray that God will break the chains,
that He will bless you and take care of you in His name.

Fear, hopelessness, and despair don't tell my story.
My honesty, obedience, and joy reveal what He has done for me.

If you have held onto fear and pain for far too long,
let go of it.
Be honest with yourselves and others,
and let God show you that *you* belong.

It's okay to show others you are weak.
Who knows, they may be more understanding than you think!

Therefore, my friend, help yourself move on today;
release the chains, own up to your mistakes, be aware of others,
take care of your heart, and last of all, put the past away!

Fear no longer has declaration in His name!

G

Gratefulness

Noun

Warm and deep appreciation for kindness received; gratitude or thankfulness

How great is our God? I am going to share some insight for those of you who haven't seen or recognized His goodness.

Have you ever felt so lonely or so far gone it feels like no one else could ever understand the depth of your pain and loneliness? I have good news for you today.

I have been there. I have experienced the lowest of lows without knowing Jesus, and it almost destroyed me. After going through tragedy, feeling lost, and losing hope in everything, I found Jesus. I say that I found Him because He has known me and loved me from the very beginning. If you feel like you are too far gone or too ashamed to give it all to Jesus, I am here to tell you that He wants you to put it all on Him. He wants to hear from you. He is ready to listen. If you have never talked to Jesus before, start by thanking Him for everything you have. You can thank Him for the roof over your head, the food you eat, your job, transportation, and the clothes you wear. Anything that gets you through day-to-day life is all thanks to Him. Once you start noticing all you have, you start noticing all He's done in your life. Jesus loves sinners, liars, cheaters, nonbelievers, skeptics, the lost, the broken, the ashamed, and the hurting. Today I want you to be grateful that it's not too late to be saved by God's grace. If you've never known God or had a relationship with Him, it's never too late to start. He craves your attention and your love. Gratefulness goes both ways. He is grateful for any time you spend with Him. We can be grateful for all He's done in our lives, and He is grateful for when we obey, follow, and listen to His wise counsel. If you've known Jesus for a long time or your entire life but have felt detached lately, thank Him today for everything you're grateful for. Write out names of people you are thankful He put in your life.

God, today I am grateful for the following people:

_____   _____

_____   _____

Journal prompt

Now, think of what you've been longing for, whether it be something you've been dreaming about or something as big as finding salvation in Jesus. Write these things out.

Be grateful, knowing that if you ask, God will listen. He will provide what you need and when you need it. If you are meant to have something, God will take care of you. If it is not meant for you, He will let it slip through your grasp. If you asked for salvation today, know that it is given to you, and you can start living the life that you've been called to live. You can let go of your past pain and hurt and start with new hope for who you are supposed to become. Do not let your past hold you back from your future. God's grace can save you and help you be grateful in the messiest of situations. Be grateful you have a Savior that is running after you every day. Don't run from Him. Let Him capture you and your heart. Be set free today.

Grateful is the person who knows God, and grateful is the God that gets to love you.

> I will give thanks to the Lord because of his righteousness; I will sing the praises of the name of the Lord Most High. (Psalm 7:17)

> Rejoice always, pray continually, give thanks in all circumstances; for this is God's will for you in Christ Jesus. (1 Thessalonians 5:16–18)

> Give thanks to the Lord, for he is good; his love endures forever. (1 Chronicles 16:34)

Let's pray

I am grateful for all of you reading this. I am grateful for all the people that picked this book up and are giving it a try. I am thankful for those of you who know Jesus and for those of you who don't. I am grateful that God doesn't judge us and doesn't ever turn us away. I am grateful God saved a sinner like me and used me to help others. I am grateful He believes I am worthy, even on the days when I don't feel like I measure up. I am grateful for the people He has placed in my life and the trials I've endured with Him by my side, for the trials have helped me grow in my faith and have shown me He is the only true light and source of my happiness. I am grateful Jesus gives us all a chance to be who He has called us to be. I am grateful for when I mess up or forget my way; He leads me back to where I belong. I am grateful for every single one of you reading this because you all have a chance to experience the life-changing love of God. Be with us, Lord, and let us be grateful for Your many blessings.

Hurt

Verb

Cause physical pain or injury to

When looking up the definition for the word *hurt*, most of them were talking about physical pain and injury caused to the outside of our bodies, injuries for which we see the doctor and ones that are usually healed by medicine, therapy, or other remedies. The hurt that I am referring to today is the deep wounds that we all have on the *inside*. We have all been internally hurt at some point in our life. It may be from grief we've experienced or something someone said about us. Hurt comes in all forms, and we are all capable of hurting others. Even the best Christians and the best people hurt others from time to time, even if it's not on purpose. We are humans full of emotions and differences, and it's impossible to walk through life without feeling hurt or getting our feelings hurt from time to time.

I have been hurt, and I know I have hurt others. What I have noticed most about hurt is, we aren't immune to it. Hurt can cause us to be someone we never intended to be. It can cause us to say words to others that tear them down. It can cause us to lose sleep at night, and it also leads to broken friendships and relationships. My husband and I experienced extreme hurt before and after we were married. But what we found was, through the hurt, we grew closer to each other. And most importantly, we grew closer to God. In time, we realized all the hurtful things that were said to us were a direct reflection of pain other people have held on to. These people were fighting far greater battles than what we could see on the surface. We stopped praying for them to stop hurting us with their words and actions and started praying God would capture their hearts and reveal their true source of pain. We wanted them to heal and live a life with freedom in God's grace. We also started praying for our own hearts to not harden toward the people who hurt us. We prayed our

27

pride wouldn't be the driving force of our pain. We asked the Lord to search our hearts and reveal anything that was not a direct reflection of Him. We did not want our pride to keep us from being godly people and doing what Jesus has called us to do. We both have fallen short and haven't always gotten everything right, but we do try, and we do our best to let God intervene through our situations. Our hurt caused us to dig deep and find things within ourselves that needed change and needed to be worked on. The hurt caused by others made us look inward at our own hearts. It made us think about why we were getting so offended and why we were carrying burdens others put on us. We realized we were trying so hard to fight the battle on our own; we forgot Jesus was ready to fight with us. He was ready to save all hearts involved. And in His power, we know there is true restoration and hope for a better tomorrow.

> Be kind and compassionate to one another, forgiving each other, just as in Christ God forgave you. Follow God's example, therefore, as dearly loved children and walk in the way of love, just as Christ loved us and gave himself up for us as a fragrant offering and sacrifice to God. (Ephesians 4:32; 5:1–2)

> Do not take revenge, my dear friends, but leave room for God's wrath, for it is written: "It is mine to avenge; I will repay," says the Lord. On the contrary: "If your enemy is hungry, feed him; if he is thirsty, give him something to drink. In doing this, you will heap burning coals on his head. Do not be overcome by evil, but overcome evil with good." (Romans 12:19–21)

When others hurt us, often our first instinct is to get revenge, justice, or let them have a "piece of our mind." Before knowing Jesus, this is what I thought was right. I thought, if someone hurt me, I should tell him or her exactly how it made me feel. I did not speak any of this with love. My words hurt them just as much as theirs hurt me. It was an unhealthy cycle, and the problems were not solved. After learning how Jesus loves, I am constantly reminded that when someone hurts my husband or me, it often has much more to do with him or her than us. We are called to show grace and only let wholesome talk come out of our mouths. Ephesians 4:29 reminds us, "Do not let any unwholesome talk come out of your mouths, but only what is helpful for building others up according to their needs, that it may benefit those who listen."

There were so many times we wanted to respond to the hurtful words of others. The more we stayed silent, the more God worked in our hearts and in our life. Others may never understand, but Jesus held our tongues and healed our hearts.

> Bear with each other and forgive one another if any of you has a grievance against someone. Forgive as the Lord forgave you. And over all these virtues put on love, which binds them all together in perfect unity. (Colossians 3:13–14)

Jesus forgave the people who hurt Him most, and He has forgiven every one of us. *Do not let your hurt stand in the way of your healing.* Do not let the pain others inflicted keep you from the purpose God has planned for you.

I know some of you have experienced unimaginable hurt internally and externally. I pray you will give Jesus the hurt you feel so you can heal and be made whole again. Letting go of the hurt frees *you*. It does not hold the other person any less accountable for their actions, but it puts you on steady ground. It frees you from their grasp and puts Jesus in control of your heart, not them. Let the hurt go. Release it in Jesus's name. Pray for their hearts to change. Pray for your heart to change. Pray for awareness so you don't hurt others the way you've been hurt. Pray for guidance and wisdom as you navigate the future.

Pray for freedom for all involved. Most importantly, pray God will reveal anything to you that may be hurting others, and pray you can forgive those who have trespassed against you. Our Lord is a mighty healer, and hurt has no victory here.

Journal prompt

Today, I encourage you to write a letter to the person(s) who has hurt you. Write exactly how you feel. Then I want you to write out a prayer to God to help you release the hurt from your heart, and ask Him to help you forgive. After you write this letter, I want you to tear the page out of your journal and throw it away. Sometimes writing things out on paper helps to serve as a release of emotions for us. Throwing it away keeps us from hurting someone else with our words. God knows your heart, and He will heal it if you let Him.

Now, let's pray

Write a prayer asking God for whatever you need, whether it be forgiveness, help to forgive someone else, or His grace. Ask Him for what you need today.

I   **Importance**

Noun
The state or fact of being of great significance or value

In your life right now, what are the five most important things to you?

① _____

② _____

③ _____

④ _____

⑤ _____

Is God on your list? If so, write down what number you wrote Him on. _____

I am sure you know where I am going with this. Do not feel bad if you did not write Him down or didn't put Him on your number one spot. I hope you didn't write Him in the number one spot just because you knew that's where I was heading with this. I want you to be honest with yourself while you work through this book so you can recognize the areas of your life needing improvement. If you put God as number one on your list today, I pray it always stays this way, and you understand the importance of Him being number one in your life.

What does God's Word say about the importance of spending time with Him and the importance of prayer? Let's take a look.

> One day Jesus was praying in a certain place. When he finished, one of his disciples said to him, "Lord, teach us to pray, just as John taught his disciples." He said to them, "When you pray, say: 'Father, hallowed be your name, your kingdom come. Give us each day our daily bread. Forgive us of our sins, for we also forgive everyone who sins against us. And lead us not into temptation.'" (Luke 11:1–4)

Do you pray every day? I hope so. But if not, let's start today. Use this verse above to help guide you. Ask God to provide what you need to live, and pray He will forgive your sins and transgressions. Pray He will help you forgive those who have trespassed against you. Ask Him to reveal anything to you hindering your relationship with Him. Pray He will guide you in the direction you should go so you don't lean on your own understanding. Our minds can deceive us and lead us to places that attempt to destroy us. Keeping an open line of communication with Jesus helps us to not fall in the traps that Satan sets for us and helps us to keep peace in our life.

> Does a young woman forget her jewelry, a bride her wedding ornaments? Yet my people have forgotten me, days without number. (Jeremiah 2:32)

We are always in a hurry. We always have something or someone needing our attention. We are constantly worrying about tomorrow and racing as fast as we can through life.

Slow. Down. My. Friend.

The only thing you *need* to do is take care of yourself and spend some time with Jesus. All the other things in your life will fall into place. *We get so caught up in the busyness of our lives; we don't carve out time for the one who gave us life.*

From here on out, I encourage you to spend at least fifteen minutes in Jesus's Word every day. Whether it's by journaling, praying, or reading the Bible, make time for it and see if your life starts changing and becomes less hectic. My guess is, you will notice a peace you haven't felt before, and it will bring you satisfaction you've been searching for. Next time you feel like scrolling through your phone or watching a TV show, try spending time with Jesus instead. The more time you give Him, the more freedom you have from the demands of this world.

> Come near to God and he will come near to you. Wash your hands, you sinners, and purify your hearts, you double-minded. (James 4:8)

> I am the vine; you are the branches. If you remain in me and I in you, you will bear much fruit; apart from me you can do nothing. (John 15:5)

Let's pray

Jesus is the most important person in my life. And because of that, I have been blessed with peace, surpassing all understanding. This does not mean I don't have hard days or days where the stresses of this world try to overcome me, but it does mean I have a source of joy I can always run to when my tank is running low. I searched for years to fill a void in my life that caused so much destruction, pain, and grief. I turned to things that brought me despair and more anxiety than I could possibly deal with on my own. Jesus is important. His love encompasses a multitude of sins, and He forgives each and every one of us if we ask Him. Jesus, I pray we make you a priority every single day. I pray we remember the importance of everything You have done for us, and let us seek You and the peace You give us when we have a relationship with You. You have been running after us our entire lives; let us embrace it and enjoy the life-changing love you have to offer.

Journal prompt

Today, in your journal, write out what you will commit to doing this week. Here are some things to try if you need some help getting started.

- ★ Read your Bible for fifteen minutes every day. Pick any chapter and start. You don't have to necessarily start in Genesis. I recommend reading the gospels (Matthew, Mark, Luke, and John) if you need a good starting place.
- ★ Pray when you wake up every morning and before you go to sleep.
- ★ Worship Him on your way to and from work.
- ★ Pick a verse out of the Bible every day, and start journaling. I like to use the SOAP method: *s*cripture, *o*bservation, *a*pplication, *p*rayer. You can even go back and pick out any of the scriptures I have referenced so far.

J

Judgment

Noun

The ability to make considered decisions or come to sensible conclusions

This word instantly floods me with emotion and hurt. Being judged or hearing the opinions of others is something that keeps me up at night. This is something I constantly have to work at and remind myself that Jesus is the only one who can judge my life. I am sure many of you have been judged and have judged others too. We all make assumptions and give our opinions from time to time. What we don't realize is how those assumptions or opinions can severely hurt the person on the receiving end. In my experience, if we judge or make an allegation about someone, we don't usually expect them to hear about it or know what we have said. Look at the definition of judgment again. When you make judgments about someone, do you really use sensible conclusions? Do you gather evidence from all sides and their past and everything they've been through and then make your statement? I am guessing the answer is no. On the other hand, I doubt anyone judging you is doing this either.

Judging is so easy to do but so destructive. I have been judged throughout my life. At just eight years old, I was judged after losing my earthly father because I didn't know how to interact with kids my age. I have been judged for making poor decisions in my past. (Likely, these judgments were fairly accurate, but they still hurt.) I have been judged for following God, for being a wife, and for simply being who I am. At the end of the day, not everyone is going to like me, and not everyone is going to like you. This was hard for me to really wrap my mind around, and I still let it bother me from time to time. There are always going to be people who judge us. Opinions will be formed about us by others, sometimes through miscommunication and misconception. We cannot control what others think.

And the sooner we realize that, the happier we will be with who we are and who Jesus has called us to become.

> Do not judge, or you too will be judged. For in the same way you judge others, you will be judged, and with the measure you use, it will be measured to you. Why do you look at the speck of sawdust in your brother's eye and pay no attention to the plank in your own eye? How can you say to your brother, "Let me take the speck out of our eye," when all the time there is a plank in your own eye? You hypocrite, first take the plank out of your own eye, and then you will see clearly to remove the speck from your brother's eye. (Matthew 7:1–5)

This verse really hit home for me. If you read it and live by it, you should never judge anyone ever again. That sounds difficult, doesn't it? Let's try putting it into practice and see how it changes our hearts.

Is there someone you have judged or have an ill opinion of? Write their name(s) down below.

_____

Journal prompt

Write out why you have judged them or why you think the way you do about them. Maybe they have hurt you, judged you, tried to hurt your reputation, taken something from you, or harmed you.

Let's pray

Write out your own prayer in your journal. God is listening, and He is near.

Refer back to *Matthew 7:1–5*. Does it resonate with you differently now after writing your thoughts out? I hope it does. The only judgment that truly matters is the one that Jesus makes about us on judgment day. As you go about the next several weeks, try to think about what you are saying and speaking. If it doesn't lift others up or benefit them, do not speak it. Keep your opinions, judgments, and biases to yourself, and let God hear them so He can heal your heart from thinking things that do not glorify Him.

The day we start judging less, we start loving people more.

Kindness

Noun
The quality of being friendly, generous, and considerate

> So in everything, do to others what you would have them do to you, for this sums up the Law and the Prophets. (Matthew 7:12)

> Therefore encourage one another and build each other up, just as in fact you are doing. (1 Thessalonians 5:11)

Have you ever heard the saying "kindness can go a long way"? There is so much truth behind this statement.

In our life, we will experience trouble and heartache, but how we react and deal with it is what truly matters. Typically, when someone hurts us or something unfortunate happens to us, we respond with anger, sadness, bitterness, or even hatred. What if, instead of these negative responses, we responded with kindness at all times and in all situations? Sounds like a perfect world, doesn't it? Being kind in harsh moments is one of the hardest things to do because, as humans, we often seek vengeance, justice, or even retaliation. Kindness takes self-control. Most importantly, it takes you surrendering your situations to Jesus so He can help you through it.

Journal prompt

Have you been in a situation where you didn't react the way you wished you would have? Write about it, and then write how you wish you had responded.

We can't go back and change the past or undo things that have already happened, but we can change the future and how we react to future issues and disturbances in our life.

If you are reading this and have a heavy heart about a past situation, remember that Jesus is here to take that burden from you.

Here are some tips to help you move forward and move closer to being kind in every moment:

1. Apologize to whoever you responded to in a negative way (if you are able to).
2. If the person does not accept your apology or responds with adversity, pray and ask God for forgiveness and to help you love them anyway. Let Him step up and do the rest of the work.
3. Write down what has been bothering you and any ill feelings you have toward the person that you had this encounter with.
4. Pray and ask Jesus to reveal anything about your heart that is unclean or impure.

I believe that kindness doesn't always come naturally in the heat of a hard situation. Kindness is something we have to choose every single day. In reality, there will be days when we don't respond kindly to a situation, but it's how we handle the aftermath that counts. Do you grow from it? Do you try and do better the next day? Do you apologize more quickly than you have in the past? *Growth happens when you start recognizing your poor behavior in the midst of it happening or, better yet, before it ever gets to that point!* Kindness happens when we let go of our pride and our own expectations and let Jesus speak through us in any and all situations. It takes time and discipline. If you spend time in Jesus's Word every day, you will start to learn what a forgiving God we serve, and He will teach you about compassion, empathy, and kindness. Remember, when someone hurts you or attacks you personally, it often has nothing to do with you and a lot more to do with them. How beautiful would it be for them to see Jesus in your response instead of judgment?

Let's pray

Lord, today help us to seek kindness. You have been so gracious to us and have given us so much. Help us to give back to others with cheerful hearts. Help us to serve and love others the way You have loved us. Let us be kind in the hard moments. Soften our hearts in the moments when we have a hard time showing kindness. Let us not judge others but be kind in all we do. Kindness is something we choose, so open our hearts to strive to be better for ourselves and those around us.

L Loneliness

Noun
Sadness resulting from being forsaken or abandoned
The state of being alone in solitary isolation

> I will not leave you as orphans; I will come to you. (John 14:18)

When we think about loneliness, we think about being by ourselves with no one else around. Have you ever been lonely while surrounded by a room full of people? Have you ever felt lonely even though you aren't really alone? I believe the definition of loneliness can be misconstrued and causes us to feel shameful when we have feelings that don't necessarily align with the definition we see on the Internet. There have been multiple times throughout my life where I have felt lonely even when others surrounded me. I felt an aching or a longing for something I couldn't quite put my finger on. I felt shameful for having these feelings. Most likely, some of you reading this know exactly what I am talking about. We live in a world full of pressure. We feel pressure to live up to high standards, to post the right things on social media, to use our voice but not use it *too* much, to be the best at whatever we do, to fit in but be unique. There is so much pressure to be these people we were never called to be. When we strive to reach perfection, we find ourselves lonelier and more isolated than ever before. We find that the more we seek to please people in this world, the more we lose sight of who we are.

> Turn to me and be gracious to me, for I am lonely and afflicted. (Psalm 25:16)

41

I believe we naturally crave to have community and close relationships. I also believe we all crave quiet time for ourselves to recharge, regardless if we are extroverted or introverted. Sometimes I find myself fueling up everybody else's tanks but not my own. Today, take a few minutes for yourself. Take five minutes to close your eyes and just breathe. Don't think about anything. Focus on one thing that makes you happy, and don't let your mind wander off this thought. Focus on the peace and stillness within you. Remind yourself you are not alone. Taking time for yourself to recharge is important for your mental, physical, emotional, and spiritual well-being. Sometimes we feel lonely because we are moving so fast we can't see the people around us. We can't feel their presence because we are too busy focusing on the next thing. They are physically there, but emotionally we are not letting them in, causing us to feel lonely and abandoned. *Slow down.* Take some time, and evaluate what is important to you. Take time to remind yourself you are not alone, and you are loved. You have people wanting to be there for you. Let them in, and cherish the time when they are around. If this means cutting some things out of your life to make it less hectic, *do it.* The moment you start feeling alone when you are surrounded by others is the moment you can be assured you are putting too much pressure on yourself to live up to a standard Jesus never set for you. Loneliness is not a sign of weakness but rather a sign to reach out for help and let others in. Let the people closest to you know how you are feeling, and carve out time in your week to spend quality time with someone you love.

> When you pass through the waters, I will be with you, and when you pass through the rivers, they will not sweep over you. When you walk through the fire, you will not be burned; the flames will not set you ablaze. (Isaiah 43:2)

Prayer and journal prompt

Write out your own prayer in your journal. God sees you.

M

Mercy

Noun
Compassion or forgiveness shown toward someone whom it is within one's power to punish or harm

> Be merciful, just as your Father is merciful. (Luke 6:36)

> Blessed are the merciful, for they will be shown mercy. (Matthew 5:7)

Have you ever had to show mercy to someone who you really didn't feel deserved it? Have you ever had to forgive someone who never apologized for his or her actions? Have you ever shown compassion to someone who was rude to you? I am sure you can say yes to at least one of these questions. The real question is, who are we to judge? Who are we to say when someone does or does not deserve mercy? I know there are people on this earth who have done unimaginable things we find disturbing, heartbreaking, and all together wrong. I also know Jesus judges sin equally, and Matthew 7:1–5 says, "Do not judge, or you too will be judged. For in the same way you judge others, you will be judged, and with the measure you use, it will be measured to you. Why do you look at the speck of sawdust in your brother's eye and pay no attention to the plank in your own eye? How can you say to your brother, 'Let me take the speck out of your eye,' when all the time there is a plank in your own eye? You hypocrite, first take the plank out of your own eye, and then you will see clearly to remove the speck from your brother's eye."

43

That really puts things into perspective, doesn't it? Jesus did not put us on this earth to judge others. He put us here to love and show compassion to those who hurt us so we can be the change we need to see in the world. As Christians, we are called to show mercy even if we don't personally think someone deserves it. It is not God's desire for us to hold a grudge or keep forgiveness from someone in our lives. None of us are perfect, and we all fall short of God's glory (Romans 3:23). As I write these words, I do not want you to think I am perfect or have this all figured out. Forgiveness and mercy are two of the hardest things for me to show, and I feel so guilty about admitting this. As a child of God, I should seek the good in every single person I come in contact with and let go of any transgressions that come against me. Truth is, I have been hurt by others and have let my anger, pride, and resentfulness drive how I acted toward them. It has taken some time for me to realize Jesus is the judge, not me. Although I knew this in my heart, Satan always tries to sneak in and destroy the good we have in our hearts. For all the good things Jesus teaches us and promises us, Satan tries just as hard to take it all away. When you are having a hard time showing mercy or forgiveness, remember, Romans 3:10 tells us, "There is no one righteous, not even one." Satan will try to tell us we are better, we can hold the grudge, we do not need to let it go, but Jesus reminds us that we must forgive others so that we too can be forgiven (Matthew 6:15).

Journal prompt

Write down the name of the person(s) you need to show mercy to today.

_____

Let's pray

This week, I want you to pray for this person(s) every day. I want you to ask God to help you forgive them for whatever harm they have caused. This does not mean you have to put them at the center of your life or even let them be a part of it. It does mean you need to work at letting go of the burden of carrying the hurt. These prayers will help you release them from your grasp so Jesus can take over. It is when we forgive that we are set free. We are set free from shame, regret, doubt, guilt, and anger when we forgive someone who we feel has trespassed against us. Show mercy today, and make the decision to commit to prayer every day this week for this person that is on your mind as you read this. I also want you to remember, when you forgive others, Jesus forgives you for your sins. When we let go of our need to control and the grudges that keep us stuck in one place, Jesus steps in and does what only He can do. His mercies are new every morning, and He is waiting for you to give it all to Him.

> Because of the Lord's great love we are not consumed, for his compassions never fail. They are new every morning; great is your faithfulness. (Lamentation 3:22–23)

Neglect

Noun

The state or fact of being uncared for

> Though my father and mother forsake me, the Lord will receive me. (Psalm 27:10)

> Do not neglect your gift, which was given you through prophecy when the body of elders laid their hands on you. Be diligent in these matters; give yourself wholly to them, so that everyone may see your progress. Watch your life and doctrine closely. Persevere in them, because if you do, you will save both yourself and your hearers. (1 Timothy 4:14–16)

There are two parts to today's letter. We will start with unpacking what Psalm 27:10 is telling us. Have you been abandoned by a parent or caregiver? Have you ever felt betrayed by your parents/caregiver(s)? If you have, this is for you. I am guessing the majority of us have felt hurt by our parents or caregivers at least once in our life. There are some people who were abandoned at a young age or abandoned later in life. Although I cannot imagine ever doing this to a child, God does not call us to judge them, and He definitely doesn't want us to carry the burden of their choices. Parents and caregivers are humans. They are not perfect, and they *will* make mistakes. When they do, God tells us we can lean on Him, and He will take care of us and give us what we need in those moments. He also tells us in Ephesians 4:32 that we must forgive others so we can be forgiven too.

Some of you have gone through unimaginable pain caused by someone else who is supposed to love you and protect you. When they fail you or have failed you, remember, God is there. God is your protector. God is your healer and hope. If you don't have a relationship with Him yet, it's never too late. Admit to Him you have sinned and have fallen short of His glory. Let Him know you believe he died on the cross for you, then commit to following Him for the rest of your days. When people hurt us, God heals us. Try to not let painful wounds of the past cause chaos in your future. You are enough in God's eyes, and that is what is important.

The second Bible verse I shared today discusses the gifts that God gives us as Christians and followers of Jesus. If you are following Christ, there is a really good chance you have a spiritual gift, and you are aware of what it is. For me, I believe he's given me a gift in my writing. I've written several different pieces over the last fifteen years, but it was not until my midtwenties that I decided to start sharing with others. I was hesitant because I was afraid others might not like what I had to say. I learned quickly that some people won't like what I have to say, or they may have different values/opinions than me. My voice is a gift given to me from God, and I am choosing to honor Him by using it to hopefully reach others.

In Matthew 18, Jesus tells the parable of the lost sheep. A shepherd left the ninety-nine others in search of one lost sheep. I knew I had to stop being scared of what everyone else thought because I might just speak to the one that Jesus intended for me to reach. God rejoices more over the one lost sheep than He does over the ninety-nine that did not go astray. If you feel God is calling you to use your gift, ask Him to open your mind, heart, and soul to what He is calling you to do. Ask Him for guidance and provision. Ask Him to walk with you as you start to share your gift with the world. Do not neglect what He is calling you to do.

If you have felt neglected or abandoned or need guidance on what your spiritual gift is, ask God today to reveal your gift to you, and ask for Him to heal the innermost parts of you that are hurting.

Prayer and journal prompt

Write out your prayer in your journal. God loves you and wants to hear from you.

O Optimism

Noun

Hopefulness and confidence about the future or the successful outcome of something

Are you an optimistic person? If you are, write down three things that help you to be optimistic.

(1) _____

(2) _____

(3) _____

Do you struggle with being optimistic? Are you more of a gloom-and-doom type of person? If this is you, write down three reasons you struggle to be optimistic. Whether it's past hurts or trauma, being let down, or not having hope, put the reasons down on paper today.

(1) _____

(2) _____

(3) _____

For the most part, I would say I am an optimistic person. I try to be hopeful and confident each day, but I recognize this is not always the standard I hold myself to. The three things that help keep me optimistic are God and His love for me; my husband and son; and my friends and family, who encourage me. In hard times, I try to

49

remind myself how blessed I am to know God, to be loved by Him, and to be loved by the people He has given me. There are inevitably days I don't have an optimistic outlook, and I really struggle to see the good. My past hurt often overwhelms my mind, and Satan tries to pull me back to where I used to be. People who are unloving and who gossip or say hurtful things have also caused me to struggle with optimism in certain situations. I have learned, over time, regardless of what anyone says or thinks, it is only God who can tell me who I am. God is the only voice in our life who gets to speak into our hearts. If you are someone who really struggles with finding the joy in each day, start reading God's Word. At first it may not resonate with you. But the more you read, the more you will start to understand. You will realize God is our ultimate source of hope and joy, and *He* is the reason we can be optimistic, even in the hard times.

Jeremiah 29:11 states, "For I know the plans I have for you, declares the Lord, plans to prosper you and not to harm you, plans to give you hope and a future."

Jesus gives us everything we need to be optimistic each day, regardless what comes our way.

> Weeping may stay for the night, but rejoicing comes in the morning. (Psalm 30:5)

Here are three steps you can take to start feeling more optimistic each day:

1. Spend time in God's Word. Whether it's ten minutes or an hour, make time for it each day.
2. Each day, write down *one* thing you are grateful for. As you get in the habit of this, start writing two things, then three, then four, etc.
3. The moment you start feeling anxious or hopeless, pray. If you've never prayed before, start now. God does

not care what your prayers sound like; He just wants to hear from you.

Prayer and journal prompt

Write out your prayer in your journal.

P

Potential

Adjective
Having or showing the capacity to become or develop into something in the future

There is a time for everything, and a season for every activity under the heavens. (Ecclesiastes 3:1)

Have you ever wondered what your purpose was here on earth? Have you ever questioned your potential and felt you were unworthy of anything good? If so, I am here to tell you that you were made for a purpose. You have potential, whether you're eight or eighty-eight, and you have the power to change your story at any given time. Obstacles get thrown at us every day, and sometimes it's not easy. Sometimes life pushes us down more than it lifts us up. When we are constantly defeated or feel we can't get ahead, we lose sight of what's to come and any hope of a better future. The beautiful part of living a life for Jesus is knowing He created us all for a purpose, and it's never too late to live out your potential.

Growing up, school came easy to me. I didn't have to study very much, and I rarely opened a book. I enjoyed school. I realize now that I probably enjoyed it because I didn't have to put much effort into it. My brother, on the other hand, had to work at school and study hard to get to where he is today. It didn't come as easy to him. The reason I am sharing this with you is because, even though my brother and I are different in this way, we both have potential to become who we want to be and have the knowledge and skills to serve out our purpose here on earth. My brother is now a successful business owner, and I have my clinical doctorate degree in my specialty. We took different paths, but both took hard work, and we believed in ourselves and the potential within us.

If you are reading this and have given up on your potential for growth in your life, I am here to tell you it's never too late. God doesn't give up on us, so neither should we. Is there something you've always wanted to do that you have always held yourself back from? Think about what is stopping you today from doing what you love. Is it finances, time commitment, supplies/resources, or just a lack of confidence?

Journal prompt

Write out something you've always wanted to do and haven't or something you strive to do in your future.

Every day that passes is another day of putting something off that could potentially change your life. Use your potential to change your purpose! If you aren't who you want to be, change it. If you aren't where you need to be, change it. If you don't know your potential or your purpose, seek God's guidance and ask Him to reveal it to you. Work hard at becoming better. Work on developing yourself into the person you've always wanted to be. Write down your goals and work toward them. If you put in the work now, someday you will look back and see that you had potential all along. You just needed the push to put it into action. Start using your potential to live out your purpose, and stop holding yourself back because of the fears that you or others have placed on your heart. You are ready, and you are able!

Let's pray

Write out your prayer in your journal. Remember, God sees the good in you.

 # Quietness

Noun
Absence of noise or bustle; calm

Be still and know that I am God. (Psalm 46:10)

This is a tough one for me personally because in the quietness, I often am overcome by dark thoughts that lead my mind astray. The quietness opens up my mind to thoughts of my past, to pain I've felt, to transgressions made against me, and to my failings and wrongdoings. I have always struggled with silencing my own thoughts and listening only to what Jesus has to say to me. Over time, I have gotten better at listening to God. I have disciplined myself to put bad thoughts on paper so I can let Jesus speak clearly to me to remind myself that those thoughts are not from Him. All of these unwanted thoughts would fill my headspace, so I was unable to listen to God and hear what He was trying to say. If you struggle with this, I am here to tell you that you are not alone. Jesus is patient and loving, and He will wait for us. It's in the quietness that I found my soul was disturbed by so many worldly things. It's also where I found Jesus and healing. Sometimes the voices in my head were so loud I couldn't focus on what Jesus had to say to me. The more I recognized this, the more I realized the things He had to say were far greater than what I was saying to myself. It was in the quiet moments with Jesus that I learned the most about Him and who I am through Him. I learned He doesn't hold on to the past, and He doesn't hold anything over my head. I learned He is gracious and just, and His timing is perfect. I learned that although I haven't always been who I've wanted to be, it's not too late for me to live out my purpose that He has always had planned for me.

Today, take some time to sit in quietness with Jesus. Find a quiet space, and sit in stillness. At first you may realize you start thinking about everything you need to get done, or all the to-do lists in your head start swirling around. You might start thinking of a situation that has you on edge or about something you aren't proud of. When these thoughts start creeping in, start praying. It doesn't matter what you pray or how you pray, just start talking to Jesus, like you were talking to a friend. Tell Him what is on your mind. Tell Him everything that needs to be done, and tell Him about your day. This may seem pointless, time-consuming, or even unnecessary, but I assure you, if you start doing this every single day, it *will* change your life and your heart little by little. *You will start silencing the voice in your head and start listening to the voice in your heart.* You will stop focusing on all you have to do and start focusing on all He has done. It's in the quietness with Jesus we learn who He really is and who He's called us to be. It's in the quietness that we start learning about ourselves. We find strength to change the narrative we've been telling ourselves for so long. The quietness pushes out the darkness, the unwanted thoughts, and the fear of changing.

The quietness frees us from the loudness of this world.

Prayer and journal prompt

Write out your prayer in your journal. Be still, and let God into this time. Let Him speak to you. Write out anything you feel He is telling you.

Regret

Verb
To feel sad, repentant, or disappointed over (something that has happened or been done, especially a loss or missed opportunity)

> Godly sorrow brings repentance that leads to salvation and leaves no regret, but worldly sorrow brings death. (2 Corinthians 7:10)

Journal prompt

When you read this definition and verse, did something come to your mind? Is it something from your past or present that is weighing heavy on your heart? Write it out.

I hear people say all the time, "I don't have regrets" or "no regrets." I believe people associate regret with weakness and shame, so they do not accept that a part of them has things they wish they could change. I don't live in regret, and I don't let it become part of my everyday routine. But there are things in my life I wish I could undo or go back and have another chance. There are things I am not proud of and things I have repented for. There are times I've held myself back from something that could have served a great purpose in my life. Instead of letting these regrets fill my soul to the brim, I give them to Jesus. I ask for His forgiveness and His provision moving forward. I ask for guidance and wisdom so I don't repeat the same mistakes, and I seek His counsel moving forward each day. We can learn from our mistakes and the chances we didn't take so we can make better choices in the future. In order to do this effectively, we have to spend time with Jesus.

Regret can leave such emptiness in our soul and can have a profound effect on our lives. We all have things we wish we could change, but life keeps going and moving, and so we also have to. We have to keep working on becoming better versions of ourselves each day that God gives us. When we repent to God, He forgives us.

Let's pray and repent

Today, spend time repenting to Jesus. Invite Him into your heart, and seek His provision. Ask Him to reveal anything to you that is not honoring Him. Don't live your life in regret of things you wish you could change. Be proactive, and start working from the inside out. Jesus can change your heart and your life if you let Him.

Sorrow

Noun

A feeling of deep distress caused by loss, disappointment, or other misfortune suffered by oneself or others

> And I heard a loud voice from the throne saying, "Look! God's dwelling place is now among the people and he will dwell with them. They will be his people, and God himself will be with them and be their God. 'He will wipe every tear from their eyes. There will be no more death' or mourning or crying or pain, for the old order of things has passed away" (Revelation 21:3–4).

Grief and sorrow are tricky, complicated, messy, and not very enjoyable emotions to feel. No person wants to grieve or experience loss. On earth, we cannot escape death, and we cannot stop bad things from happening. It is likely, many of you reading this have experienced the loss of someone you love. If you haven't lost a loved one, you have probably experienced the loss of a job, a relationship, a future you thought you were going to have, or even the loss of who you thought you were going to be. Grief can come in all different forms, and it is very complex. Grief comes in waves, and it is not linear. It's a process. No two people will grieve in the same way.

Losing my dad at eight years old shaped me into the person I am today. I struggled for many years with doubts, insecurities, and hardships. I was lost and had no sense of hope for my future. I longed to find wholeness and wanted so badly to stop hurting all the time. My life was changed after I found Jesus and started reading about the hope He gives us. I still grieve and have days that are harder than others, but I have a sense of purpose, and I am fulfilled by the love only my heavenly Father can provide. Having a relationship with Jesus when I had my miscarriage in January 2024 changed how I grieved. I was still very sad, but I had hope for my family's future. I had someone to lean on who I knew would never leave my side. I had trust in Jesus that His plan was better than mine. I still grieved because I lost someone, but this time instead of feeling lost and alone, I felt seen and loved through my hurting. My greatest prayer is for each of you reading this to know Jesus so when sorrow inevitably happens, you have hope through your pain.

Journal prompt

Are you grieving right now? What is in your heart that is causing pain and sorrow in your life?

Now I want you to write three things you are thankful for.

① _____

② _____

③ _____

You are allowed to be happy, to be loved, to enjoy life, and to experience the beauty in this world. You are also allowed to cry and have bad days. Just remember, for every bad day you have, you can probably recall at least three good ones. I like to call this the *three-to-one rule*. One day may get you down, but the three other days you can recall will lift you up. Try it. There is good in all of your days if only you will look for it. When you are feeling sad, write down three things you are grateful for. You will find beauty, hope, and grace among your grieving when you start looking in the right places. In times of darkness, suffering, agony, and hurt, remember, the Lord will bring you peace in that moment and in the days to come if you call on Him.

The following poem is a tribute to my dad, a wonderful man who people often tell me I remind them of, a man who never knew a stranger, a man who loved his family deeply and passed away doing what he loved. September 7, 2002, dismantled our lives, but today I am confident in saying that God has pulled me from the darkness and given me a hope that can only be found in Him.

Grief Is

Grief is painful,
Hard,
Frustrating,
Never-ending,
Challenging,
Heartbreaking,
Earth-shattering,
Life-changing.

Grief is what made me, me.

Some days I'm really strong, and some days
it's hard to find where I belong.
Grief has taught me many things, but it has
never brought you back to me.

We live each day on earth, longing to see your face,
and someday again I'll enjoy your sweet embrace.

Grief doesn't end, and it never goes away,
but it will teach you everything you need to
know about being thankful for each day.

Grief can take you one of two ways.
One is moving forward, and the other will lead you astray.

I have chosen to move forward and be
thankful for the times we had.
You were my very favorite and incredible dad.

I will refresh the weary and satisfy the faint.
(Jeremiah 31:25)

The Lord is close to the brokenhearted and saves
the crushed in spirit. (Psalm 34:18)

Let's pray

Write out your prayer, and give your burdens to Jesus today.

Who You Are Right Now

Who you are right now is not who you will always be.
Who you are right now is just the grief, you see?
Your pain and hurt are overwhelming,
but Jesus promises new mercies in the morning.
Don't let others make you feel like you aren't enough.
Truth is, most people haven't gone through this hard stuff.
Who you are today is a person who is stronger than the day before.
Who you are tomorrow
is a person holding on for so much more.
There is hope around the corner.
There is joy that is near.
But, my friend, you have to feel it all to heal.
Who you are in the midst of your grief doesn't define you,
but who you are right now in this season is beautiful too.
The messiness, the hurt, the anger, the sadness—
eventually you'll be able to smile again with gladness.
In the in-between and the healing of your grief,
remember, God made you stronger than you think.
Who you are today is someone with incredible strength.
Who you are today is someone within God's reach.
Who you are today is someone who has experienced loss and pain.
Who you are today is not to be felt in vain.
In the end,
aren't we all so much the same?

The following poem is a tribute to our baby in heaven.

Carry You with Me

I miscarried you today.
It's like I slowly watched you fade away.

I held you in my heart from the very start.

When I saw those two blue lines, I was a little
worried about having two babies back to back.
But I knew, God would fill in everything I lacked.

I felt like we went on a rollercoaster today. My emotions were
up and down, and I feel I lost a little of myself along the way.

My comfort is knowing you are safe in Jesus' arms.
You won't know pain or hurt and from my heart, you'll never be far.

I am grateful I knew about you,
even if it was for a very short time.
I am so glad God let you be mine even if
it was only for a little while.

I will remember you when I choose to find joy in each day,
I will remember you when I choose to appreciate
all the things that come our way.
I will remember you for the sweet innocent baby you were.
I already loved you, even before I knew if you were a him or a her.

Although I miscarried you today,
I will continue to carry you with me for all my days.

T

Temptation

Noun
The desire to do something, especially
something wrong or unwise

> No temptation has overtaken you except what is
> common to mankind. And God is faithful; he
> will not let you be tempted beyond what you
> can bear. But when you are tempted, he will
> also provide a way out so that you can endure.
> (1 Corinthians 10:13)

Do you struggle with temptation?

○ Yes

○ No

Do you feel convicted if you give into temptation?

○ Yes

○ No

Temptation is when Satan is trying to keep you in the dark. It's not a glamorous statement, but it's the truth. Satan has one job: It is to tear you down and keep you there. God has an even bigger job to lift us out of the darkness and into His light. We are tempted every single day, and every single time God gives us a way out. We can try to deny the way out or the opportunity God gives us to not be tempted, but that doesn't mean He didn't provide a way. We often give into temptation because it's easier than saying no or being different than how others believe we should be.

I have struggled with temptation just like most people do. There were times in my life I wanted to fit in or be liked by people who didn't have my best interests at heart. After several years, I really started to wrestle with my feelings of guilt and conviction whenever I would make a choice that I knew was not pleasing to God. I would feel heaviness in the days following my choices, and it would wreck me. I would fall on my knees and pray for forgiveness. *Each time, God picked me up, set me on my feet, and reminded me it was Him I was living for, not them.* The world tells us to do things to fit the mold. God tells us to do things that break the mold. Don't put yourself in a box just because others have put themselves in one. Be different, and choose what makes your heart free. Choose to obey God, and listen to what He is saving you from. The next time you are tempted and you have that small voice in your head, reminding you of the right thing to do, choose what you know is right. If you start listening, you will start truly living. It is not giving up all the good things in life but rather gaining everything better that only God can offer us. Temptation is Satan's way of making things appear to be better than God's grace and His plan for our lives. The more you start saying no to temptation, the more fulfilled you will be.

Journal prompt

Write down the areas in your life where you are most tempted. Write out the things or people that tempt you.

If you have never felt conviction after making choices that don't reflect God's Word, start by praying and learning who God is. The more you center your life around what He says, the more you start to understand how much He loves you and wants the best for you.

Let's pray

Lord, I thank You for each person reading this today. I pray You will release the chains of temptation that we have bound around us. I pray You will be with the people who are struggling to say no. Please wash clean the sins and mistakes we have made. Please forgive us for the ways we have displeased and dishonored You. Please forgive us when we choose this world over You. Please light a spark in the people who are feeling discouraged by the ways they have been tempted in the past. Let them cling to Your Word and the truth that You speak. Breathe life and light into their lives, and remind them they are loved regardless of their past mistakes. If the person reading this has not felt conviction for their choices, please capture their heart in this moment and give them discernment. Please place people in their life that are a true reflection of Your love. Help us to set boundaries and stray away from people encouraging us to engage in things that do not lead us closer to You. I pray we start focusing more on our eternal life than the life we have on this earth. Please be with those who are hurting, and forgive those who cry out to You. Set us free from the temptation and turmoil of this world, and let us serve You in every way we can.

> I am coming to you now, but I say these things while I am still in the world, so that they may have the full measure of my joy within them. I have given them your word and the world has hated them, for they are not of the world any more than I am of the world. My prayer is not that you take them out of the world but that you protect them from the evil one. (John 17:13–15)

Uniqueness

Noun
The quality of being the only one of its kind

> For you created my inmost being; you knit me together in my mother's womb. I praise you because I am fearfully and wonderfully made; your works are wonderful, I know that full well. (Psalm 139:13–14)

It is easy to compare ourselves to others, and we often find ourselves wishing for things other people have. There are seasons of our lives where we strive for different things or want more than what we currently possess. What if we stopped focusing on what we don't have and started focusing on what we do? God has made us all unique in His image. He has made all our lives different for a reason. Some people may have more money, some people may have a better career, and some people may have more friends. The list goes on and on. The reality of this list is, it is all based on opinion.

Who defines how much money is enough or a lot? Who defines what career is better than another? Who tells us how many close friends is the perfect amount? Who tells us which house is the best and trendiest? Who defines the best clothing?

The answer? *No one.*

No one on this earth has the correct answer to any of these questions because it is all based on opinion and the uniqueness of each individual. Society has tried to tell us what is best or what we should have. If we always listen to the norms of society, we will fall short with despair every single time. Instead of focusing on how we are different or lacking, let's focus on what we have to offer. We all have a unique gift or trait we can share with others. We have to be confident in what God has given us, and we can't live our lives comparing everything we do to those around us.

Journal prompt

Write three traits you like about yourself or gifts/talents you can share with others.

① _____

② _____

③ _____

Now choose one and try to focus on it this week. Remind yourself God gave you this ability or gift, and He can use it. Be confident in its uniqueness to you and how God designed you to be.

> Your hands made me and formed me; give me understanding to learn your commands. (Psalm 119:73)

Let's pray

Write out your prayer, and ask God to reveal to you what your gifts are if you are unsure. If you feel you know what gift God has given you to share, pray He will guide you in using your gift to bless others.

V

Vulnerability

Noun

The quality or state of being exposed to the possibility of being attacked or harmed, either physically or emotionally

But to you who are listening I say: Love your enemies, do good to those who hate you, bless those who curse you, pray for those who mistreat you. If someone slaps you on the cheek, turn to them the other also. If someone takes your coat, do not withhold your shirt from them. Give to everyone who asks you, and if anyone takes what belongs to you, do not demand it back. Do to others as you would have them do to you. If you love those who love you, what credit is that to you? Even sinners love those who love them. And if you do good to those who are good to you, what credit is that to you? Even sinners do that. And if you lend to those from whom you expect repayment, what credit is that to you? Even sinners lend to sinners, expecting to be repaid in full. But love your enemies, do good to them, and lend to them without expecting to get anything back. Then your reward will be great, and you will be children of the Most High, because he is kind to the ungrateful and wicked. Be merciful, just as your Father is merciful. (Luke 6:27–36)

There is *a lot* to unpack with these verses. If I had to sum up what His Word says in this passage, I would say, Jesus calls us to love those who persecute us, and He calls us to be merciful and forgiving, rather than spiteful and guarded.

When someone hurts us, we often put a wall up around our heart and guard it with everything we have so we don't get hurt again. As humans, we do not like to feel suffering, and we will go to extreme measures to protect our hearts. Jesus tells us, when someone hurts us, to do the exact opposite. He says, if someone slaps us, let them slap the other cheek too. *Can you truly imagine?* Most of us are reading that statement, thinking we would never let someone hit us and then hit us again without doing anything about it. This is where vulnerability and humility come in. When someone slaps us or hurts us, retaliating serves no purpose and only causes more harm. If we let them hit or take from us, and we step back and don't put a guard up, we show them a love that they may have never seen or experienced before.

I am sure some of you reading this can't imagine not standing up for yourself when someone comes against you. If you truly think about it, the world has taught us to fight back, to make our voices heard, to stand our ground. If you read Jesus's Word, He never tells us to put our guard up around people who have hurt us. He wants us to be vulnerable in a good way. He doesn't want us fighting and retaliating. He doesn't want us to stand our ground when it could potentially hurt others (even if they hurt us first). This doesn't mean we allow someone to continuously hurt us, but it encourages us to love them anyway. The more time we spend with Jesus, the more comfortable we will be with showing vulnerability to other people. This doesn't mean you have to share your life story or be their best friend. It means you will show them forgiveness, mercy, and grace and move on. You will not become guarded because of their choices and actions. You will show mercy like Jesus has shown to all of us. You will be vulnerable enough to let Jesus be exposed through you and how you handle tough situations.

If there is someone in your life who has hurt you that you cannot even fathom being vulnerable with, write his or her name here.

_____

Today, I want to pray for these names we have written above. I want to pray for our hearts to change toward them so we can let the walls come down around our hardened hearts.

Let's pray

Lord, we come to You, asking for you to show us how to be vulnerable in a good way. We don't want to let people walk all over us, but we want to extend grace as much as we possibly can. We want our hearts to change toward the people who have hurt us so we can love them the way You have loved us. We want You to help us see them through a godly lens. For people who have been hurt so badly that they can no longer be around the people they have listed above, I pray for their hearts to not harden. I pray they will forgive this person. Remind them that You forgive us when we forgive those who have done us wrong. Help us to be vulnerable enough to keep our hearts open to You and what You ask of us. Lord, protect our thoughts and keep us from conforming to this world. We ask You to have mercy on us and to help us show Your mercy to others.

Letting Go

There comes a time when you have to let go.
You have to let go of everything you know.

Let go of the past that has broken you in places;
let go of the pain associated with familiar faces.

Let go of the hurt and heavy burdens that cause so much dismay,
and trust God will lead you on your own way.

Trust that God has a much bigger plan,
one that is stronger, greater, and more powerful than any man.

Do not let anyone tell you who you are.
The same God that made you, made the stars.

The people who have dimmed your light and caused so much pain,
those same issues may still remain.

Although the same issues are present and hurt really bad,
you have to look at your blessings and all that you have.

Do not focus on the one that brings you down,
but look up to the one that gave you the
ability to smile and not just frown.

This life and this plan may be different than you ever imagined,
but if you trust God, He can give you more
than you could ever fathom!

Choose to hold on to those dear to your heart,
the ones who lift you up,
the ones who love,
the ones who support.

Be thankful that God has given you another day.
For those against us, we pray and know that
in time God will make His way.

Worry

Verb
Give way to anxiety or unease; allow one's mind to dwell on difficulty or troubles

Worry comes from Satan. It's as simple as that. There is not a single thing in this life we should worry about, yet we find ourselves worrying almost daily. Sometimes we worry about small things, like what we are going to wear. Sometimes we worry about bigger things, such as our future or the outcome of a painful time we are enduring. Our minds naturally tend to worry. If we don't have knowledge of God and Scripture, we can be overcome with anxiety.

I have struggled with worry most of my life. It started when I was a young girl, and over time it manifested into a very big problem. I would constantly worry about the days to come and if something bad might happen. I would worry about pleasing others and what others thought of me. After I lost my dad, I let worry consume me. I was worried something would happen to someone else I loved. *I would worry about worrying.* It consumed my mind, my heart, and my life. It affected my relationships and caused an abundant amount of unnecessary stress. It wasn't until my twenties that I realized I had a severe case of *lack of faith.* When I went to college, I was surrounded by Christians and people who had a relationship with Jesus. I found myself being envious of how happy they all seemed to be. Of course, none of them were perfect, but they had a joy in them that was undeniable. I began to seek the Lord and started asking questions to anyone who would listen. The more I learned about Jesus, the less worried I became. I realized, after just a short time of knowing Him, He was faithful and would carry my burdens if I let Him.

I still worry and have bad days, but they are much fewer than the early years of my life. Worry is a choice, and if we let it, it will take over our minds. Worry causes us to doubt God's faithfulness, and it brings chaos into our hearts and lives. Worry makes us focus on everything that could go wrong, so we stop believing that anything could go right. Worry steals our joy and our peace. It serves no purpose in our life. A question I would often ask myself is, "How is worrying going to change my situation? I never had an answer because worry can't change anything. *God changes everything.* It took me a very long time to get a handle on my worried thoughts. It took years of studying God's Word and memorizing Scripture so I had verses to recite to myself when anxious thoughts tried to take over. I still struggle from time to time, but I am thankful I have a weapon now against Satan's attacks. Satan wants to steal all of our peace. Don't fall into his trap, and don't believe the lies he is telling you. God's Word is the only thing that is true, and He constantly reminds us in the Bible not to worry. Listen to Him, and let Him be the strongest voice in your head. Below, I am sharing Bible verses that are helpful to commit to memory. These are verses to repeat to yourself when you start feeling anxiousness creep in. Our battles with Satan can only be fought with Jesus's Word.

> Who of you by worrying can add a single hour to your life? Since you cannot do this very little thing, why do you worry about the rest? (Luke 12:25–26)

> Do not be anxious about anything, but in every situation, by prayer and petition, with thanksgiving, present your requests to God. (Philippians 4:6)

> He gives strength to the weary and increases the power of the weak. Even youths grow tired and weary, and young men stumble and fall; but those who hope in the Lord will renew their strength. They will soar on wings like eagles; they will run

and not grow weary, they will walk and not be faint. (Isaiah 40:29–31)

Do not let your hearts be troubled. You believe in God; believe also in me. (John 14:1)

When anxiety was great within me, your consolation brought me joy. (Psalm 94:19)

Prayer and journal prompt

Write out your worries today. Let God in this space so you can feel His peace.

XO: Hugs and Kisses

When God put it on my heart to write this, I instantly started worrying about the letter *X*. I find it ironic because I just wrote about worry in the last section. As we all know, there are not a lot of common words that start with *X*. I searched and searched but didn't find what I was looking for. One day, I started writing, and the thought came to me to use this letter as a time of reflection.

XO usually represents love, and we write it on cards, texts, and letters to people we hold dear to our hearts. I am truly thankful for all of you who have read this and worked through it. I pray that your hearts have been opened to God and His Word, and I pray this helps grow your relationship with our Lord and Savior.

To my loved ones, especially my husband, I could not have done this without you. You encourage me every single day by the way you love me. You lead me closer to Jesus, and you push me in the best way possible. You are selfless and humble, optimistic and loyal, and good for my soul. The Lord gave me a great gift in you. To my son, you have shown me a love I never knew I needed and a love that surpasses words. Having my own child has shown me so much about Jesus's love for all of His children. I love others better because of you. You are such a light in our world. To Rebecca Smith, a mentor and friend, you have given me so much wisdom, insight, and love in the time I have known you. You challenge me and encourage me to be the best version of myself. You redirect me to Jesus in all our conversations, and you lend advice that I will cherish forever. I pray someday I can be the person you are to me to someone else. To my mom, thank you for everything you sacrificed for my brother and me. Thank you for growing with me over the years and for always loving me. To my friends and family who have supported me and encouraged me to keep writing, *thank you*. Your support means everything to me.

Journal prompts

- ★ What have you learned from doing this devotional?
- ★ What is something you feel you have *gained* from doing this devotional?
- ★ What are three things you are thankful for today?
- ★ Who are the people who encourage you the most?
- ★ Write out a Bible verse from this devotional you want to commit to memory.

Who Will You Choose?

When the world is calling our name,
everything will always remain the same.

When we say yes to the world,
we say no to God.

God can promise us eternity.
The world offers us uncertainty.

When you are given the choice to choose this world or God,
will you choose Him?

The walls of this world can come caving in,
but with Jesus, you always have a protector and friend.

Yearning

Noun

A feeling of intense longing for something

If I had to choose one word to describe how I felt in my adolescent years, this would be it: yearning. I yearned for so much more than what life was at that time. I yearned to be set free from my sinful nature and the brokenness I felt in my heart. I yearned to be the person I knew I could be. I yearned to be forgiven. I yearned to be set free from hurt caused by others and myself. I yearned for something greater than myself. The best part about my story (and yours too) is Jesus is walking with you even when you don't know it. He knew you when He knit you together in your mother's womb (Psalm 139:13). At the time when I was searching for something bigger, I had no idea the area of my life Jesus had already begun a great work in.

When I was eighteen years old, I left for college, and God placed several Christians in my life; my husband included. There was something different in all of the people I encountered, and I wanted to know what it was. The more I learned about them, the more I learned about Jesus. The people I met not only loved Jesus, but they had a relationship with Him, and their life reflected this. The first time I ever got on my knees and prayed, I dreamed about my dad for the very first time since his passing. God sometimes shows up in small ways or through other people. I truly believe He gave me this dream to show me He was listening. I knew then I had to keep talking to Him. My life was changed after this. A few years later I was saved and baptized, and my life was completely changed. I am still a sinner and fall short of God's glory every day, but I found the hope I was yearning for. I found forgiveness through my Father in heaven, and I found grace. I am still learning how to live my life as a direct reflection of Jesus, but I am thankful for how far I've come.

Are you yearning for something more in this life? If you are reading this and don't have a relationship with Jesus, please use this time to pray and ask Him to show you who He is. Praying can sometimes feel awkward at first, but the more you do it, the more you notice someone listening on the other end.

Journal prompt

If you don't have a relationship with Jesus, what is keeping you from it?

Don't get bogged down by the rules of the Bible. Jesus wants your heart. He will change you and search you once you let Him in. He isn't here to ruin our lives or take good things from us. He is here to comfort, protect, and guide us through this temporary home. There is not a single thing in this world that can compare to Jesus's love. Temporary things are like Band-Aids; they may fit over and cover a small wound so no one can see it, but eventually the wound gets bigger if we don't care for it properly. Band-Aids are temporary and so are the pleasures of this world. Our wounds only get bigger and more painful the more we use temporary things to fix them. Let God in, and see the transformation for yourself.

If you know Jesus and have a relationship with Him, I am so grateful. I am grateful He has captured your heart and you've seen His goodness is far greater than anything this world has to offer. Now that I have a relationship with Jesus, I am always yearning for more. Yearning for more grace and forgiveness to show others, and more understanding to love people who are different than me.

Is there anything you need to give up or stop doing to help your relationship grow stronger with Him?

Second Chronicles 14:7 says, "'Let us build up these towns,' he said to Judah, 'and put walls around them, with towers, gates and bars. The land is still ours, because we sought the Lord our God; we

81

sought him and he has given us rest on every side.' So they built and prospered."

> I long to see you so that I may impart to you some spiritual gift to make you strong—that is, that you and I may be mutually encouraged by each other's faith. I do not want you to be unaware, brothers and sisters, that I planned many times to come to you (but have been prevented from doing so until now) in order that I might have a harvest among you, just as I have had among the other Gentiles. (Romans 1:11–13)

Today we will end in prayer, and I invite you to ask Jesus to come into your heart if you feel led to do so.

*A*sk Jesus to enter your heart.

*B*elieve Jesus died on the cross for you and your sins.

*C*onfess your sins and commit to a relationship with Him.

See what I did there with the ABCs.

Let's pray

Lord, we come to You today broken, misled, and yearning for something greater than ourselves. Please forgive us for our sins and the temporary things in this world we have used to replace You at times. Please lead us in an understanding of who You are and the sacrifices You have made for us. Be with those who are praying this prayer today who don't know You. I pray You will reveal Yourself to them in mighty ways and capture their hearts so they don't ever want to look back on their old ways. Lead those of us who know You and seek You daily. Help us to be better stewards of Your Word, and help us to show Your grace and mercy daily. Thank You for all You have given up to have a relationship with us. Thank You for the healing You have brought into this broken world. Thank You for reminding us this is our temporary home. Let us yearn for a greater hope in You and our eternal life.

Z

Zealous

Adjective
Marked by fervent partisanship for a person, a cause, or an ideal: filled with or characterized by zeal

To be zealous is to be *passionately in favor of.*

I believe Jesus wants us to be zealous for Him. It is actually stated in the Bible several times. I will share verses below supporting this. He wants us to crave a relationship with Him and wants us to share His love with others. He doesn't want to only live in our hearts, but He wants to capture other people's hearts through ours. He wants to change us so we can help Him change the broken world we live in. I believe he wants us to passionately seek Him and constantly work on our relationship with Him. I truly am zealous for the Lord and everything He has to offer. My life with Him is far more peaceful than when I tried to do everything on my own. I look forward to my daily quiet time with Him. I am always eager to learn more about who He is and all He has done for you and me.

> Never be lacking in zeal, but keep your spiritual fervor, serving the Lord. (Romans 12:11)

> Those whom I love I rebuke and discipline. So be earnest (zealous) and repent. (Revelations 3:19)

> For I can testify about them that they are zealous for God, but their zeal is not based on knowledge. Since they did not know the righteousness of God and sought to establish their own, they

> did not submit to God's righteousness. Christ is the culmination of the law so that there may be righteousness for everyone who believes. (Romans 10:1–4)

Jesus wants you in His life. Jesus does not judge you for what you have done. He asks that you repent and earnestly seek Him with all your heart. It is *never* too late to have a relationship with Jesus.

If doing this devotional has led you closer to God or opened your heart to who He is, I would love to hear from you! You can email me at plummernik@gmail.com.

Often we read through a devotional, go to a conference, or hear a good word preached, but there is no follow-up. I believe people get lost in knowing what to do next and find it easier to give up than to search on their own for the next steps. God placed people in my life who have changed my life and led me closer to Him. If I can be that person for any of you, I will gladly take on that mission. I want you to know you are not alone in anything you go through, and our God is greater than anything you will face on this earth. Thank you for picking this up and working through it. I believe God has given me these words to share, and I believe He will use each of you who have picked up this book.

Let's pray

My prayer for you is that you know how loved you are. You are loved in the beginning, middle, and end of your pain and suffering. The messiest parts of you are nothing for Jesus. He is not scared or fearful of the baggage you bring when you lay down your life to Him. He is not going to judge you or turn away from you for your past and your sins. Jesus laid down His life so you could have yours. Start focusing today on all the good. Start looking for the joy and goodness in your day. Start reading your Bible. Find people to connect with in a local church. Step out of your comfort zone, and start becoming the person Jesus has called you to be. If He can call me out of the darkness and use me, He can use you too. Thank You, Jesus, for every single person who has picked this up. Thank You for letting them *want* to know You more. Thank You for their commitment to this and to You. Thank You, Jesus, for giving us hope in such a broken world.

Journal prompt

Below, I would like you to write down three things you are committing to work on in the days to come or three things you are willing to give up in order to have a closer relationship with Jesus.

① _____

② _____

③ _____

Let Jesus use you and transform you. There is no better time than right now.

Now that we know our ABCs, next time you encounter the enemy, pray to Jesus and watch Him work in your life, just like He did for me.

Thank you for being here, friend.

I'm praying for you as you go on your way.

About the Author

Dr. Nikki Plummer grew up in a small town in Nebraska. She lost her dad when she was eight years old. This left Nikki and her brother to be raised by their mom. Nikki spent most of her adolescent years searching for something to fill the void she felt in her life. That void was filled when she encountered and started following Jesus in college. Nikki received her doctor of audiology degree in 2020 and thoroughly enjoys  serving people through her career as an audiologist. However, she feels her greatest accomplishment thus far is becoming a child of God. Without Him, she would have nothing. She is now married to a wonderful husband that God placed in her life, and together they are raising their son. Nikki is passionate about sharing the gospel so others who might feel lost or empty may come to know Jesus too.

Printed in the USA
CPSIA information can be obtained
at www.ICGtesting.com
CBHW021920131024
15803CB00034B/314